GRAND CANYON

North
Rim

South Rim

Colorado River

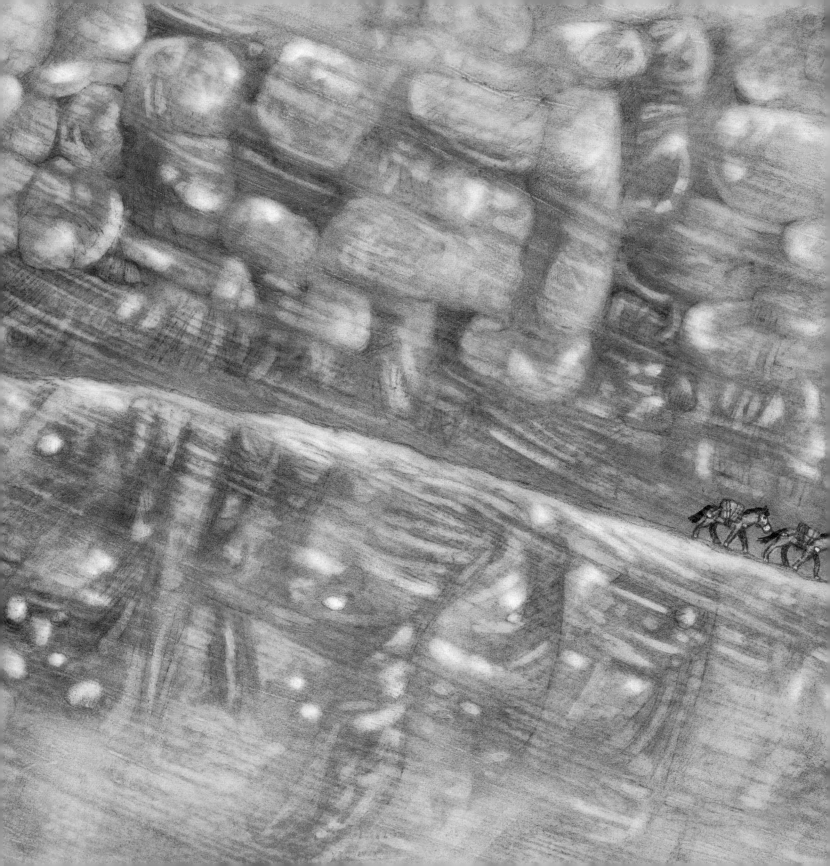

Mule Train Mail

Craig Brown

ini Charlesbridge

Anthony the Postman doesn't wear a uniform.

He wears a cowboy hat, chaps, and spurs.

Anthony doesn't drive a mail truck. He drives a mule train. He picks up the mail at the south rim of the Grand Canyon.

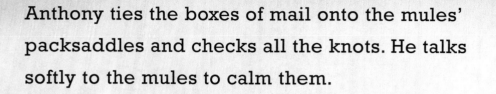

Anthony ties the boxes of mail onto the mules'
packsaddles and checks all the knots. He talks
softly to the mules to calm them.

The mules carry letters and packages, along with
groceries, water, clothes, and even computers.
During the holidays they deliver everything
from pumpkins and turkeys to Christmas trees.

When the boxes are loaded, Anthony waves his lariat and calls out, "Hi-ya!" The mules start moving along the dusty trail.

The mule train has a long way to go.

The canyon floor is more than one mile below.

Anthony zigzags along sharp switchbacks.

He rides across high plateaus.

Sometimes he stops to look.

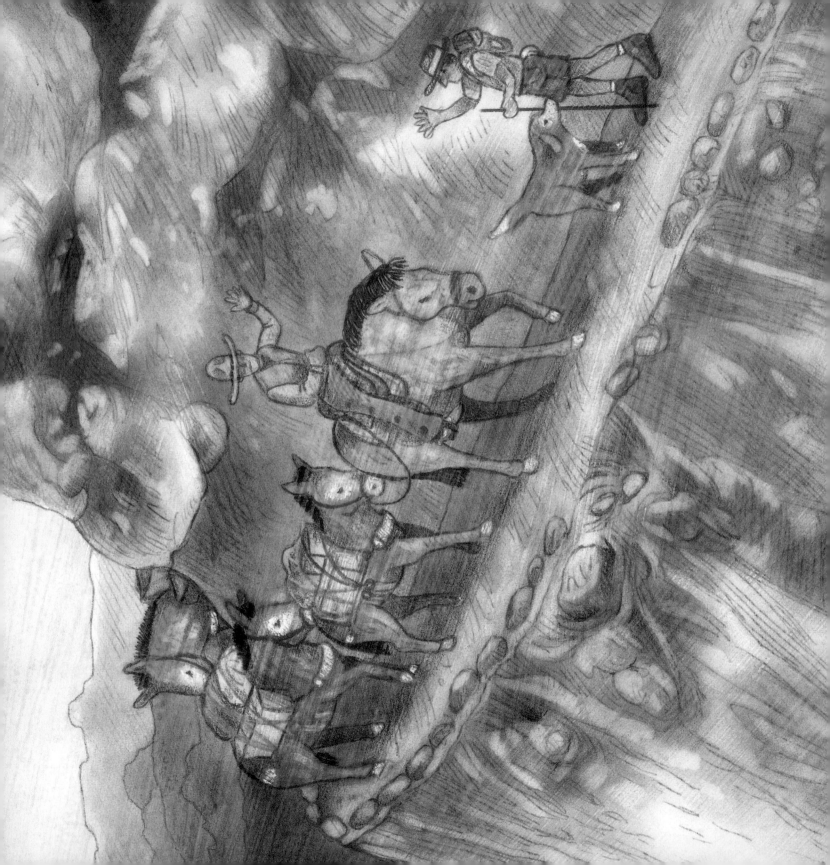

The trail is steep and narrow. Anthony and his mules carefully squeeze past hikers.

They pass the bones of a mule that had fallen from the trail.

Some days the trail is slick with mud. Slippery ice is the most dangerous. But the trip has never been canceled, in spite of rain, sleet, hail, and flash floods. The mail must go through.

At last the mule train reaches the canyon floor.
Anthony follows a dry riverbed as it snakes
between high sandstone walls.

It is hot in the canyon. When the mule train reaches Havasu Creek, Anthony lets the mules take a quick drink from the crystal-clear water.

Anthony and his mules continue on their way
in the shade of old cottonwood trees.
Soon they can see the village of Supai,
tucked into a lush valley beneath steep red walls.

This is home.
The mules' ears perk up,
and they walk faster.

Anthony leads the mule train into the village.
He calls out, "Whoa!" and the mules stop outside
the post office. He scratches each mule behind
the ears.

Villagers greet Anthony as they come to pick up their mail. Anthony's wife and five sons hurry to meet him.

Then Anthony the Postman and his family
walk home with the day's mail.

Author's Note

Mail by Mule

The village of Supai is located on the Havasupai Indian Reservation at
the bottom of the Grand Canyon. The only ways in or out are by foot,
horse, mule, or helicopter. Since 1896 the mail has been delivered
by mule train. Led by a skilled muleteer, the mules make the eight-
mile trip from the top of the canyon to Supai in three hours. The mule
trains encounter obstacles from 100-degree heat in the summer
to ice, mud, and freezing rain in the fall and winter. Despite these
hazards, the mail has never been canceled because of weather.

A Trip into the Grand Canyon

As an author and illustrator, I take pride in presenting books that
have been accurately drawn and researched. For this book, I knew
I had to take a trip into the Grand Canyon with the mule train mail.

With my son and a friend, I began the trip by following a mail truck
from the post office in Peach Springs, Arizona, to the south rim of the
Grand Canyon. There we met Anthony Paya, lead muleteer. Anthony
tied the boxes of mail onto the mules, speaking to the mules in his
native Havasupai. When the team was ready to go, we mounted our
horses and followed Anthony into the canyon.

Looking straight down at the switchbacks, I felt a fear I hadn't experienced in some time. I had to trust my horse to place each hoof safely, which he did. Soon I was able to relax and take in the rocks, plants, clouds, and vistas. My head kept swiveling back and forth, as every direction offered an inspiring view. The scenery and colors were an artist's delight.

As we reached the canyon floor, the vistas were replaced with gigantic rocks and high sandstone walls. We snaked along a dry riverbed, sometimes riding through narrow ravines where we had to duck to avoid tree limbs and rock outcroppings. Leaving the riverbed, we came to shimmering Havasu Creek. After three hours in the saddle, we found the water cool and refreshing.

Back on the trail my anticipation grew as we rode between giant cottonwoods and entered the village of Supai. The houses were neat, with gardens and swing sets. In place of cars and garages were mules, horses, and barns. This was definitely a world unto itself.

We watched as the mail was unloaded at the post office. Soon villagers arrived to pick up their letters, groceries, and other packages—their supplies from the outside world. Thanks to Anthony and the other remarkable muleteers, the mail had once again gone through.

To Isaac: Books are fun and allow us to dream the impossible. *—Love, Grandpa Mac*

To photographers and travel mates Cory Brown and Doug Potter: Thanks for the laughs and photo memories.

To Hank Delaney, Connie Olson, Terry Misenhimer, and Larry Moore: Thanks for your support.

Special thanks to muleteers Anthony Paya and Darren Siyuja for a beautiful and exciting adventure.

Text and illustrations copyright © 2009 by Craig Brown

Published by Charlesbridge
85 Main Street
Watertown, MA 02472
(617) 926-0329
www.charlesbridge.com

Library of Congress Cataloging-in-Publication Data
Brown, Craig McFarland.
    Mule train mail / Craig Brown.
        p. cm.
    ISBN 978-1-58089-187-5 (reinforced for library use)
    ISBN 978-1-58089-188-2 (softcover)
1. Mule train mail—Arizona—Grand Canyon—Juvenile
literature. 2. Mule train mail—Arizona—Supai—Juvenile
literature. 3. Postal service—West (U.S.)—Juvenile literature.
I. Title.
HE6239.M85B76 2009
383'.143—dc22   2008007252

Printed in China
(hc) 10 9 8 7 6 5 4 3 2 1
(sc) 10 9 8 7 6 5 4 3 2 1

Illustrations done in pastel and colored pencils on gessoed
 Strathmore paper
Display type and text type set in Estro and Rockwell
Color separations by Chroma Graphics, Singapore
Printed and bound by Regent Publishing Services
Production supervision by Brian G. Walker
Designed by Diane M. Earley